Sacred Intimacy

Sacred Intimacy

Walking Through the Forbidden Doors

Rocky Romeo, B.A. M.A. O.B.O.D.

To order additional copies of this book, contact:
Xlibris Corporation
1-888-795-4274
www.Xlibris.com
Orders@Xlibris.com
69280

CONTENTS

DEDICATION

I would like to dedicate this book to three of my wonderful instructors and friends. I'm sure that if I named the first one, an international speaker and teacher, he would not welcome it because he very much prefers to remain in the background, anonymous whenever possible. I can remember asking for a photograph with him and he wouldn't stop walking, then, turned a bright shade of red. Nevertheless he has helped me to grow and discover myself. Here's to you in hopes we meet again soon.

Thank you Kelly, for being there for all of us when we needed you. Let's talk again soon.

Dan Millman has inspired millions of people with his series of books based upon his original Way of the Peaceful Warrior. I had the privilege of taking several classes with Dan and he has become a wonderful leader for me and a good friend. Thanks so much Dano.

AUTHORS NOTE

I am still amazed and bewildered at how many people have read this book and only focus on the physical journeys. Then, they distort what it means and add their own fears and prejudices and the next thing you know, OMG!! Doing so actually illustrates and reinforces the need to add real intimacy in our lives and to keep each moment precious and sacred. Intimacy is not sex (surprised?) although physical loving is one window or door that can lead to intimacy. There are many other doors as well. Since most people involved in a committed relationship have physical relations, this book uses that window or door to inspire them to discover what real intimacy means. Yes, it's a challenge however most of life is comprised of challenges. What is essential is that awareness is being created. In some aspects, you will be examining yourself from the inside out and that can be frightening. Seeing yourself in a truthful mirror can frighten even the best of us.

I've also illuminated my own challenges and personal journeys. I did this to give you peek at what I've experienced first-hand and what thoughts were challenging me at the time. Sacred intimacy can change your relationships for the better if you can see the big picture and allow yourself to open to both your partner and yourself.

PREFACE

This is a book about you. Your life. Your nature. Your spiritual path. This is a book which will change your life forever. More and more each day, our human nature and our divine spiritual path become ever more repressed and confused. We are praised at work and home for multi-tasking. Women are encouraged to be able to do it all, care for all, and still be sexy and bring home the bacon. Men must be leaders, plumbers, gardeners, lovers, auto mechanics and more. The more we do, the further we get and the more money we make. If there is ever a time when we finally catch up on our work or home, the mantra is then "super multi-tasking" will solve everything. Our brains are becoming machine like by always being pushed to the limit. Most everyone's stress is higher than just a few years ago as we commit a slow death by trying to keep up with machines, our wife, our children, our husbands and even the "Jones". You're probably thinking that all of this is voluntary right? Think again. Technology is forcing us to keep up, re-learn, throw out, survive or die. For example, we listen to radio (a single task). We watch television listen to and watch television (double task). We can now listen, watch and read television (the written banners flashing under the CNN News broadcasts). If you've played video games, you can add movement to the mix. Cell phones, iPods and videos follow us everywhere. Some people cannot bear to turn off their cell phones when even when they eat, sleep or use the restroom. Texting among teenagers has become increasingly popular and the need to stay connected, in my opinion, overrules the essentials of daily living. No wonder we can't seem to devote ourselves to a single task anymore or even the most important people in our life. Dare I say it, even our selves? We neglect ourselves in getting enough sleep, nourishment, spiritual and physical health. This great lack of single tasking is also taking its toll in the bedrooms across America. The need for just physical sex has now replaced the need for sex as a means of an opening to true intimacy.

I commend you for purchasing and reading this book because YOU want to re-claim true intimacy in your relationship and have a more fulfilling spiritual and loving journey. The good news is that it's not too late to do this no matter what stage your relationship is in. I am going to show you how to discover and nurture an unbreakable bond that is so solid, it's almost impossible to break. This is what truly keeps couples together. What you will learn here, will change your relationships for the better and open your heart to acceptance, forgiveness and true love. Let's begin . . . .

CHAPTER ONE

The Oxymoron

So many things can be learned from a book. Some things cannot. Learning Karate only from a book may get you hurt or even killed. To study swimming only from the printed page my get you six feet under in murky waters. What I am hoping that this book will do is INSPIRE you to explore the needed physical and relationship exercises to increase your awareness of intimacy and challenge you to go beyond rational thought into the "feeling zone". By only reading this book without doing the wonderful exercises, you are denying yourself and your partner of the only true teacher of intimacy which is . . . experience of this exact moment. This is why I do not agree with teaching sexual techniques except for therapeutic purposes. There are no instructions here on how to find the G spot or achieve the elusive, ultimate orgasm. I'm not going to tell you use two fingers or three, kiss this or that, rub this or that. There is really only one mantra or instruction and that is to be totally in the moment wherever you are and FEEL something that may in fact be potentially pleasurable. This is so much easier said than done. Every one of my close friends said they can do this without any problem, but when it really comes down to brass tacks, they totally can't do it. It is then I hear a myriad of excuses. "What would my mamma say? What if daddy found out? What would my rabbi think if I were doing this? What would my neighbors think?" Or simply "I don't do THAT." So let's start now to embark on our "forbidden journey" towards real intimacy knowing again that the only real way to strengthen our relationships is to *Be Here Now* and just FEEL in the spirit of love and respect for all that is.

Being here now is also an oxymoron. After all, aren't we all here now in one way or another? Let me ask you this; If on your way to work tomorrow a stranger were to approach you and say "Excuse me, where are you?" Would you be able to answer that question? Are you on your way to work? Yes? Are you at the train station? Perhaps in the car and stopped at a red light? Well; where are you really? What if another stranger asked you; "What time is it?" I bet you can answer that one right? Could it be 10:15am? How about 7:00am? What's the correct answer? Did you figure it out by now? The answers will certainly surprise you. What time is it? NOW! Where are you? HERE in the present moment. That's the answer. So, where are you as we begin our journey? Be here. Be here now. Be here in a loving way. To be here now IS to be in love with your existence. Otherwise, we are all relatively here now to some degree. And finally, be here ANYWAY! Some of the exercises will get emotionally and mentally challenging. You may experience hesitation, extreme joy, and doubt, intense feelings of well being, intimacy and even fear. Regardless of what it is you feel or think, be here now and be here ANYWAY.

In learning from my mentors, in my first year of studies I didn't have a clue. There were times when I felt too challenged and too many secret emotions and feelings were now exposing me to the rest of the class. I was embarrassed and my pride was hurt. So what's a man to do? Leave. I ran out of class practically in tears as my emotions and desires took control. Luckily, my mentor was kind enough to run out of class after me and confront me. "If you run away from this moment, you'll be running away for the rest of your life like I suspect you've always done". He was right of course. When it gets too hot, I leave the kitchen so to speak. So, I returned to class and finished the entire course. I'm so glad I did. The point is that you will be challenged to review all that you may believe to be true. I'm not saying it will be easy, but it will be worth it if you can stay in the "now", in the present.

CHAPTER TWO

Learning to be here now, no matter what

Why be here now anyway? All of the things you own, all the things you are, what's the most precious thing there is? The house? The spouse? The kids? The 401K? It's none of the above. We are all born with a gift. A fragile gift that is given to us as a blessing. This gift is the gift of life, within this blessing is THIS MOMENT. NOW, HERE! It can never be captured the exact same way twice. It is not limitless but finite until life abruptly ends as we know it. Yet, we waste these moments by starving them to death with various multi-tasked events trying to turn one pure moment into two, three or four moments all at once. For example, when was the last time you were able to think of single thought for more than sixty seconds? For some, this has never happened yet. All kinds of thoughts pour through our minds like and endless sea of unfiltered garbage. So, we literally "blank out" and live our moments in a stupor of glazed over eyes and buried emotions. We have become routine and mechanical in our nature. Multitask or die.

Some moments can be joyous while others can be very painful. We all know of people who turn to drugs, tobacco and alcohol to keep from fully feeling the moment. I've even seen my neighbor load up her day with so many multi-tasking chores at work in order to keep from being alone with her own thoughts and being totally present. It's a habit now with most of us. We are more machine like than human, afraid to just be and afraid to just feel. The result is misplaced energy, a lack of "being" for ourselves and especially our partners. The termed western notion of sex is a great example of what intimacy via robotic sex has become. It is a true phenomena of the modern western world in which we live. If I were to stand up and move my pelvis back and forth in a sexual way, I would be having western style sex. My body is having sex with you (the pelvic movement) yet, I am also writing this book. Think it doesn't happen in your personal world? How many times have you had sex and your mind began to drift to the well being of the kids? Stock market? Work? the bills? It's almost impossible to stop because of our multi-tasking encouraging society. The bottom line is that when you multi-task thoughts during sex, you are denying yourself and your partner of true intimacy which can only take place in the moment, here, now. We go through the motions, do our duty so to speak and we begin the race for the big "O". If this sounds familiar, you are intimacy starved and also starving your loved one by denying them the beauty of the moment and your complete attention. Sex for many couples has now been reduced to just a physical race for orgasm. And so it goes in the life of a modern metropolitan, sex in the city couple.

When someone is sexually satisfied yet intimacy starved, they tend to keep wanting more of what they're not getting. They re-visit the door of sexual pleasure over and over again looking for something they can never seem to find. They know that one of the gateways to intimacy is sex, so they believe that opening more doors over and over again is the way to find it. This commonly takes the form of cheating on your partner and even leads some to sexual addiction. It's kind of like playing the lottery really. You could become an instant millionaire by scratching off the instant ticket, but every time you don't win, you want to play again and try another ticket yes? In reality we need be inspired to experience true sacred intimacy with ourselves and with our partner. Only when we are truly feeling and not thinking, judging, condemning, rejecting, multi-tasking and filtering can we begin to open the doors to "bliss" within ourselves and then with our partner.

Another common challenge which interferes with intimacy besides sexual and drug addiction (which helps us to feel LESS) is depression. I believe, as my mentors do, that depression is exactly what it says "de-pressed". Somewhere along our history we were encouraged to feel less, express less, be less than we can be and as a result, keep us from our true nature as human beings. The ability to feel fully and unconditionally is essential to developing sexual intimacy (emotional and physical). I'll be the first to tell you that I'm not a medical doctor or medical anything, but I believe that one way to help people who are depressed and who feel less, is to help them to express themselves and feel more. This path has more than enough of shared controversy among the medical profession, but it is something to consider and discuss with your doctor or mental health professional.

Religion has been the great repressor of sacred intimacy. Maybe this will sound somewhat familiar "the body is willing but the spirit is weak." In reality, the body cannot be separated from the spirit until death occurs. We are one. We are all feeling, human beings. Religion has encouraged us for thousands of years to feel less, stay virgin like, and suppress all sexual desires until they say its o.k. Religion is given to us as a spiritual path but it is ancillary. It is *instead* of our nature, not our true nature. To realize our true spiritual path, all we have to do is to return home to being fully human and celebrate all that we are and all that we can be. To be here now, we need to feel with our bodies and all of our senses but not through the filter of our logical mind. Not through a complex maze of filters and restrictions, rules and regulations no matter where they may have come from. To do so just suppresses true intimacy and sends it off to oblivion where we will remain our metropolitan, robotic, computerized shells of humanness.

CHAPTER THREE

Opening the first door

The first door on our sacred path to sexual intimacy is the understanding of the nature of male and female. Truly these natures seem to be changing and even merging recently. I find it rather frivolous how our culture constantly struggles to name these changes almost as fast as they occur. Transsexual, transvestite, gay, bisexual, transgendered, metro sexual, intersexes, polysexual, pan sexual, straight and alike should be somewhat familiar. Point of note: how many of these terms made you cringe, shriek, scream or condemn? If any did, you are filtering them through your own prejudices and colored glasses. Maybe it's time to stop and think of where your prejudices came from? Dad? Mom? Religion? Nationality? Culture? As for me I am not concerned if you are any of the above, a combination of the above or none of the above. I don't care if you are alien or domestic in your sexual orientation. The fact remains that we must not judge or filter thing that are potentially pleasurable with our logical minds.

Gender and gender roles have blurred but it still remains a fact that gender plays a large part in our lives. If we were to attempt to define the male nature, I would say that males "do" or instinctively "act". Males are capable of performing most any type of act, good or bad and sometimes even violent. When someone is steeped in their maleness and acts without consciousness and loving, they lack the inner caring which is intrinsic to the female nature. There is no love going on. No caring going on, just selfish acting on testosterone alone. Some claim that this is what world conflict is all about. Acting without caring, without love. In order for man to be complete and human, he must embrace certain aspects of the intrinsic female nature. Caring, loving, expressing and communicating.

The beginning of gender when we are still in the womb is quite a curiosity. We are all female in the first few weeks of our formation in the womb. We are all born of a female. A human cannot be more connected in body and spirit than to share themselves physically in the act of being born flesh from flesh. We inherit closeness to the female nature being part of our mother. To be female is to just to "be" by its very nature. A man acts, and a woman "is". A mother loves her child because the child "is" not because of what the child does or does not do. So, to deny our link to the feminine is to deny our very existence of being, caring and loving. Again, a man must embrace his feminine side to be a complete man. Still, society does not allow the freedom of a man to do so as it has allowed women over the last forty years to do with the male nature. It's not an easy thing to do, but very necessary.

Women are constantly encouraged to embrace their masculine side (to act) and rewarded when they do so. Not so the other way around. The next step for women's liberation is for them to accept the male as they have done for women. Women must investigate the thought that the equality they seek can only truly be realized when both genders are equal spiritually, politically and so on. This can translate into equal roles in sexual pleasure, intimacy and play. Keeping our singular stereotypical roles for ancillary reasons will only damage and break the bonds of true sacred intimacy. What does this mean then? It means that there really are no roles that must be played in developing intimacy. No rules that must be followed, no techniques to reach orgasm, no game plan, no expectations. No anything at all. Just FEEL and be in the sacred moments that you are given with your partner. If you can accomplish this, you will eventually see how ridiculous it really is to have expectations of what your partner or even you alone will say or do. The only thing having expectations will do is to add an immense amount of intimacy damaging pressure to your relationship. Eventually, you'll discover the utmost joy in dropping all expectations, prejudices and judgments to savor the hugging, closeness and spiritual union of two souls developing an unbreakable bond of joy.

CHAPTER FOUR

Feel the fear and do it anyway

Most definitely the biggest obstacles to sex and sacred intimacy are fears and trust. When examined, you will discover that most of your fears were given to you by someone else. Someone else told you it was wrong. Someone told you it was a sin. Someone told you it's not healthy or good girls just don't do that. Enter our parents, clergy and friends as the source for all of this. Yet, we still know deep deep down inside in the depths of our humanism that we are blessed with everything we need to feel, to love, to enjoy the essence of ourselves and others. The truth is we've forgotten how to feel and as a result let fear and logic cloud our abilities. Fear in itself breeds mistrust, hesitation, too much caution and of course, a big slice of guilt to top it all off. Don't get me wrong, logic is a good thing when we need to calculate or analyze something, but it doesn't belong in the bedroom or in any part of our sacred intimacy.

So what do we do when confronted with the unknown emotions and feelings of raw fear? We acknowledge it totally and fully. Then, thank God for allowing you to feel things you may never have felt before. Fear is not a bad thing, but it needs to be accepted and acknowledged as an intrinsic part of the process. It is perfectly natural to feel fearful. There are ways to confront fear using our physical abilities. On the physical level, breathe in deeply every time you are confronted with fear or hesitation. It's interesting to note that when people are in a state of fear, their breathing becomes short and shallow. It's a defense mechanism. If you truly want to feel less, just breathe less. In fact, if you don't want to feel anything at all, just don't breathe at all. Get the picture? So, to confront fear on a physical level, breathe slowly and deeply, and then breathe out with a shhhhh sound. The process of breathing out is always a surrender. Breathe in to feel and breathe out to surrender. This may seem like something not related to sacred intimacy but I assure you that you may need to do this as hidden emotions and fear pop up during some of the journeys (exercises) we will take. Note also that your significant other or partner may also be feeling the same fears and anxiety. You are not alone and it's perfectly natural to feel that way.

Guilt is the great nourisher of fear. So much fear is born out of guilt that our lives are drastically changed in one way or another. Guilt also leads to regret another blocker of intimacy. The fact is that we are all sexual beings in our intrinsic human nature. There is no reason to deny it, confront it, abolish it, control it or alter it in any way. Our being is a gift from God just the way it is. All we have to do is to come home and celebrate all that we are, all that God gave us. So, feel the fear and continue to stay totally in the moment. Be here. Be here now. Be here regardless. Be here anyway. Our journeys will take you step by step, one baby step at a time down the path of sacred intimacy. By doing so, the path will be gentle, exciting, liberating and blessed.

CHAPTER FIVE

Being intimate with yourself first

Our journey can be described as a sacred dance in three parts. Part one is when you are able to dance in full intimacy with yourself and no one else. Part two is being able to recognize and find someone else who is also willing to dance in the same open and loving manner. Part three is where sacred intimacy really occurs. It is when you are able to open fully to your partner and your partner to you. When this happens, a third dance is created; the dance of sacred intimacy. This is a truly blessed and sacred event. It is a level of intimacy which is generally not reached by modern, metropolitan Americans. But first, we need to begin with ourselves in overcoming our own barriers. List all of your own deepest sexual prejudices, stereotypes and alike. Now, create a second list when and where you were first aware of them. How did they come to you? Who gave them to you? How have they affected your past relationships? Your sexuality? Your masculinity? Your womanhood? Your current relationships? Do they make you feel free and exhilarated or restricted in some way? Now, let's move to what you will NOT do during intimacy. Who told you that you couldn't do THAT? What if you wanted to do it anyway? Why wouldn't you want to try something that could be potentially pleasurable? Be open in your feelings. Be loving in your approach and honor your thoughts and fears as God given. There is nothing to be ashamed of as we are all divine and God given. Every loving thing that we are is God given. Open your mind and expand your feelings. Be willing to trust in your openness. Trust yourself to feel the pleasures of love and intimacy. It is only in your own trust. Love and intimacy that the stage can be set for others to also gravitate to you in the same way. Be the love and trust and openness that you want to see in others. It is possible. It is pleasurable. It is sacred. A small mantra to develop openness is to tell yourself simply the phrase "and this, and this, and this". Most people have the opposite mantra when it comes to physical relationships and intimacy, it's "not this, not that, not this, not that." Do you see the difference? Can you BE the open one? The accepting one? The non-judging one? The one with no prejudices? I bet you would want to find a partner like that yes? Then, you need to be that person first. Only in this personal manifestation will the like attract like and the first sacred dance will begin. The following journeys will help you to accomplish just that. They will lead the way by holding a big mirror so that all that you are will become very apparent. No doubt that it's frightening to see who we really are. To acknowledge our deepest fears and emotions. However, the joys will outweigh them tenfold.

Journey One: Dancing a real dance.

Physical relationships are not the only doors to intimacy. Any act that puts us totally in the moment, in a loving and caring way can be a door to intimacy. With this in mind, we will journey on the path of Free Dancing. This can also be done with a partner or in a group; however we can just begin with ourselves for now. Wear comfortable, loose clothing. Play some exotic, rhythmic music (Asian Indian or new age is best for this). It must be rhythmic and can be medium or fast. Now begin to dance free style. As you listen to the music, close your eyes and feel every beat reverberating down deep within you. Begin to get in touch with you inner caveman or cavewoman, the raw inner human nature that knows no logic. The beauty here is to just FEEL and not think of anything whatsoever. Open your eyes and begin to dance in any manner that the music takes you. Use the elemental nature that is God given. The human nature. The raw nature. The real you! There is no pattern. There is nothing you must think of. Don't fall into any pattern or style. Like the old saying goes "Dance like no one is watching". Let yourself go totally into the music. Dance around the entire room. Try not to stand in one place. Do whatever the music tells you to do. Keep totally in the moment. Don't look at your partner (they should be dancing too). Let go. Let loose. Shout. Sing. Whatever it takes to be at one with the music. Let your primal human nature take over. Switch your brain off completely and just FEEL the music. If you have a hard time with this and are a bit self conscious, just close your eyes. Your partner can do this too if they are also feeling self conscious. (Be careful not to dance into any object if you close your eyes). Can you do it? Are you up to the challenge to let go and return to your primal human condition? I hope so. It's a good beginning. How did it feel? What does it feel like for you to be coming home? To return to your primal nature? Scary isn't it, but it is your true nature, a real return to just "being".

In the next part of this journey, we are going to free dance again, this time I want you feel what it is like to free dance as a man if you are a male, and as a woman if you are female. What moves would a man or woman make sexually when they dance? There are no pre-conceived moves. Trust in your own sexuality to allow it to blossom in all of its sacredness. There are no rules. If you are with a partner, face each other and begin to dance again for at least twenty minutes feeling the raw inner sexuality of your longing. Feel what it is like to have sexual passion and desire. Move in ways that convey your passion and inner gender. Be certain to face each other during the entire dance. This journey can be done in a group also. Have the women and men face each other in two lines about fifteen feet apart. You don't need to stand opposite of your partner, it can be with another person. Keep each gender within its own line. Dance and enjoy your sexual nature. What did you discover? What did you feel? What did it feel like this time to be in touch with your manhood or womanhood as the dancing progressed?

CHAPTER SIX

Opening the doors with someone else

We have seen what it is like to begin developing self intimacy by getting in touch with our primal, raw nature. Now, for this next journey, we need the help of a partner. This can be your significant other or even a stranger who is willing to assist you for just three minutes. When I first ventured into this journey, it was one of the most intimate things I have ever done. I was totally in awe of all the emotions, fears, defenses and other thoughts that were going through my mind. This journey is specifically made for you to see you. The real you deep down inside. The inner being that's hidden from everyone. In our society we are always hiding. We use rules to hide our emotions. We use clothes to hide our body. We use logic to mask our feelings. We even use excuses to cover up our ineptness. We hide from our children, our bosses, our mothers, fathers and even from ourselves. No wonder sex is so superficial, so mechanical, and so not sacred. It is my belief that this is a major cause of couples splitting up and ending their relationship or marriage. We have become more robotic and insensitive than ever. The path of sacred intimacy is a series of journeys to openness. To open and love with a deep heatfelt respect. Let's begin. Stand and face your partner. Walk up to them until you are both about fifteen inches from each other's nose. Keeping hands at your side don't move, just stare into each other's eyes for a full three minutes and don't move or say a word. It should be easier with a significant other, but can you do it with a stranger? How about a stranger of the opposite gender? How about with someone of the same gender? What did you feel? What were you thinking? Repeat the journey again but this time with the goal of using your eyes as a window to your soul. Not only see, but be SEEN. Show your inner self to the other person. Remember we are always opening. With a significant other, take a moment now to sit on the floor (use a pillow if you like) and share your feelings with each other. Share what you discovered on the journey about yourself, about them.

Until now, we have taken several journeys toward sacred intimacy without ever physically touching anyone. We will continue to do so with the following amendments to the previous journeys. Repeat each of the previous journeys again, from solo free dancing all the way to the looking into eyes, but this time do it sky clad (dressed only in the sky) naked if you will. How do you feel about that? Are you afraid of your nakedness? Shy? That's perfectly fine. Say "hello" to all of your feelings. Befriend it. Make friends with it. In going sky clad, remember to breathe into feelings and breathe out your surrender to them. If you feel self conscious again, close your eyes for a bit and just be with your inner self. We seem to be the only species on the planet that is ashamed of our nakedness. Ashamed to be open with or without our clothes. In my teachings I usually invite everyone to become sky clad after experiencing several journeys. It is always an invitation and never a requirement. It's just another way to be more open with each other and be in touch with our human nature. The bottom line is to be open in your nature with or without clothing; to show more of our inner and outer selves.

When we deal with others in our lives, the issue of trust may come into play. Should we trust our significant other? Can we trust a stranger if they were participating in the previous journeys with us? The answer is that if we are indeed fully present in the spirit of love and respect (both people) then the foundation for trust exists. Otherwise, how long do you have to know someone before intimacy can occur? One month perhaps? How about two years? Maybe, three days? It varies for everyone, but? It's not about a length of time it's about what's in your heart. For those who can't see what's in their own heart or the hearts of others we design requirements and filters for intimacy. So, how many years must one be married before they REALLY trust their partner? Filters and requirements can disguise themselves as a specific type of clothing, length of hair, height, weight, eye color, even political status. The truth is if we are love, none of the above is needed. What is love? Love is the acceptance of someone's basic human nature. You may not like all that they do, but you essentially love all that they are. It intrigues me to wonder how many of us have trouble with intimacy and love when for the most part we can't even seem to describe in some fashion. Yet, in its purest form love is beyond words and beyond our capacity to define. It is the realm of the sacred, the mystery, and the spirit. Knowing this is the intimacy in your life fulfilling or is it partial? Let's continue with a new journey.

Journey four: Setting up a sacred space at home

Ideally, having a sacred area of the home can enhance the experience tremendously. Some may argue that having a planned space makes things so unsponteneous and therefore unfulfilling. Rest assured because sacred sex will create spontaneous intimacy. We are only dressing up the window so to speak. What passes through that window will be spontaneous and thrilling. Above all the sacred place must be as safe as possible so that no life is threatened or danger of sickness exists. You may want to dress the area in soft pillows, fragrant incenses or perhaps the scent of fresh flowers. Candles add a wonderful and sacred atmosphere and can be used most anywhere. If candles are not permitted by law or if they present a risk of fire, substitute flameless candles instead. Yes Virginia, they even make scented flameless candles these days. Check on-line or at the local chain home furnishing stores. Needless to say (so I'll say it) your sacred space should be free from cell phones, alarm clocks and other everyday distractions that keep us out of the moment. We are making a conscious effort to disconnect from the electronics and other distractions that attract stress. Music is an important addition and played gently in the background will amplify the senses. Choose music played on natural instruments, native instruments. This is a complete 180 degree turn from the Hollywood notion that love should be made with disco, rap, or the top fifty pop music in the background. Remember, we are returning to our real human spirit that has been lost in the modern world, the real you, the raw and passionate you. This is the you that is open, willing and ready for intense pleasure. By the way, bedrooms can make a wonderful sacred place if dressed up a bit. Finally, allow sufficient time to experience your partner fully and completely. This is not a race to orgasm or a race to anything else. It is a sacred journey to be cherished and respected.

Preparing the space is one essential step. The next step should be to prepare ourselves. A warm leisure bath or shower which works wonders to relax us and prepare our "gift" for giving. Dress the body in not only intimate attire but also spiritual attire to show respect and honor to the divine. Perhaps add earthly symbols, a plant sprig, flowers, natural beads or scents. Come together in the prepared sacred space and honor the presence of your partner by putting the hands together in a praying form and slightly bow the head in recognition of their presence. Lovingly take each other's hand and say a short but relevant blessing of the sacred space and the sacred intimacy to follow. At this point, the moment can take over and sacred sex can begin. If a more detail is needed for inspiration, you may try sitting across from each other

in a comfortable position, using pillows if preferred but no chairs. Begin by both closing eyes and feeling the energy enter the body with each slow, deep breath. Smell the aromas and begin to let the music become part of your body. Open your eyes and see each other with complete openness as man or woman. Begin to lovingly sense the feelings of touch both inside and out. Look deeply into each other's eyes and sway sensually with the music (still seated). Let the rest be spontaneous, in the moment and perfectly natural. Do not multi-task, judge, or have any expectations whatsoever. Be totally in the moment. Give the moment you have and play joyfully within the soul of your partner. Let the door of sacred sex be open and the dance of sacred intimacy begin. Let go of all time and distractions and bask in the richness of all that the divine has given us.

When finished, lovingly thank the divine together by blessing the sacred space and giving thanks for the spiritual realm that was opened for you both to enjoy. Then, face your partner and again form the hands in prayer (Namaste) slightly bow and give thanks to each other for the sacred intimacy that was shared in love and spirit.

Now, wasn't that something different than the notion of "Hollywood" sex? What did it feel like not to rush to orgasm or have any expectations or prejudices? Did the sacred intimacy seem more significant and blessed than the normal slam bam performance sex? When the third dance of intimacy, the

spiritual dance is developed as part of sex, it becomes nourishing, fulfilling, and ecstatic with joy and playfulness. A complete 180 turn around in my opinion. Ah, I know what you're thinking. Who has time for all of this when I have kids, work fifty hours a week and have to clean the house or mow the lawn? The good news is that the sacred space once set up for the first time is pretty much ready for the next time. Besides, isn't your spiritual and sexual life worth this small effort? If our past path of sacred intimacy was really working for us as a nation, couples would not be as intimacy starved as they are. They wouldn't be trying to feel less in their lives by taking recreational drugs, alcohol and alike. They certainly wouldn't' be hiding their inner most thoughts and secrets from their significant others. I believe there would be less sexual addiction (searching for true intimacy) and less infidelity in marriage. The modern day metro couple still believes in some part that the grass is always green on the other side (with someone different) when they should be considering watering their own lawn instead Yes, it is different and out of the ordinary trend of internet age thinking but it is just a simple return to our own nature and humanity that has been sorely forgotten and covered with technology and baggage.

CHAPTER SEVEN

Variations on a Theme

Let me ask you something. Do you understand the awesome power of being totally in the moment? If so, read on. If not read the previous chapters again. Remember that it has to be experienced to foster an understanding. The moment has to be "given" by you or someone else. You can't do that by reading a book as we discussed before. It is in its creation that the moment thrives and intimacy occurs. Understanding this, is it then possible to be create intimacy with more than one person at a time? Yes, it is. Well wait a minute please! That's just plain wrong. Isn't that doing something evil? No it really isn't. If the doors of sacred sex are to be opened, they can be opened to several people at once if all are in the same spirit, understanding and respect for being in the moment. Can a person achieve the same sense of sacred intimacy if the door of sacred sex involves several people at the same time? Initially, the short answer is YES! However, you may discover that by staying with the same partner, a deeper form of sacred intimacy may occur simply because the trust becomes deeper over time; hence we open more and receive more. Sacred sex (the door to sacred intimacy) involving more than two people at once can often result in more doors being opened by having different experiences residing in the moment. It can actually be potentially pleasurable if we again can allow ourselves to be totally "here now". On the other side of the coin, you may not prefer it after having experienced it and that's totally fine. You may not prefer sacred intimacy with just one steady partner and that's just fine too. The decision is yours to make. It is your primal nature. There are no expectations, rules or prejudices. Just feel and play with all that is given to you in every moment.

CHAPTER EIGHT

Dynamic Differences

When discussing the essence of man and the essence of woman there are important dynamic (in the moment) behaviors in which to note. In a group of about thirty people there was an interesting journey of man and woman. The instructions were to slowly migrate across the room to separate areas, one for men and one for women. It was observed that the women were feeling "at home" or more comfortable with the same gender than the men were. In every group other hidden feelings may exist such as envy, jealousy, competition, admiration and alike, but for the most part the women were more accepting of each other than the men were. What could be the reason for such behavior? Is it that women are more "touchy-feely" with each other so being with other women was easy or is it something else? Upon further investigation, it was reported that once the men grouped with each other, they became occupied in glancing over the invisible gender line to visually see the women. This behavior wasn't replicated by the women. So, why the difference? The difference is that we are all born of woman. The female nature contains an intrinsic, primal connection with the birthing gender that may allow her to instantly relate on a higher level. Woman born of woman. I don't believe there can be stronger connection than to share the same gender within the same body of a human. From the masculine point of view, this connection is not present in an equal sense because the genders are opposite. Therefore when grouped together as men, we may find the longing glances towards the female side of the room as if to say "where is woman"? Where is she?" The bonds of female to female are strong. This may also explain the apparent hint of being more comfortable when asked to journey on the path of intimacy with their own gender than males are. For males, let use this metaphor. As if to list the ingredients of a recipe, let's add a helping of restrictive religious dogma, two tablespoons of machismo, ½ lb of societal laws and three helpings of parental superstitions. Stir vigorously until well blended in a soufflé of guilt and shame until you are almost powerless to come home to your real nature. Females are not exempt totally from this toxic dinner, but they do have a cushion of the woman to woman relationship. So we can conclude that the challenges of intimacy can vary with same gender journeying

There are both group dynamics which come into play and gender dynamics. Each requires a distinct path to follow in developing true, sacred sexual relationships. I work with couples, singles and even groups of strangers. They all provide a special challenge of learning to open and love in a dynamic environment. The same hold true from our earlier journey using music as a method to keep us in the moment. We will find that our thoughts differ when dancing in free form, singly, alone verses dancing with a group of strangers. And so it is also in the realm of touching within different genders and similar genders, singly and in groups. Always remember that touching can occur on the inside and the outside. If we can allow ourselves to be touched in both ways, heartfelt and physically, we are then open to the complete experience of the divine.

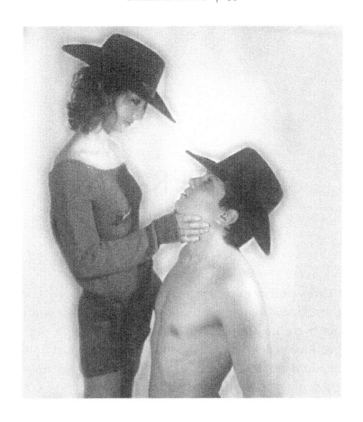

CHAPTER NINE

Into the Fire

In my early experiences with sacred sex, I entered class with an exceptional cockiness that was a result of my smug over confidence. Sex and intimacy were no strangers to me. I lived through the sixties and seventies free love generation. Now, I'm sitting on a cushioned floor of a quiet classroom nestled in the serenity of a lakeside woodland. The greenery and sounds of nature made it an ideal location so far away from metropolitan lifestyle we were all accustomed to. Roughly, I say there were about thirty adults in class ranging from ages eighteen to sixty. Some came from as far away as South America, Germany, Canada and Hawaii. The balance between male and female was about even. All of us introduced ourselves via the pass around microphone. As the classes slowly progressed from lectures to integrated journeying people's anxiety levels spiked up tremendously. It was apparent that the deep inner feelings being expressed were not only rooted in love and joy but early childhood scarring and parental misgivings. With so much individual openness being expressed it was inevitable that differences of opinions would surface quickly, and they did. So many of us were wounded and mislead by our neighborhood peers. It was very clear that our wonderful teacher had his hands full with student psychological and physical differences surfacing left and right at every turn. This confirmed to me the real reasons that we are intimacy starved and generally unable to experience the spirit, the sacred. Because of his heartfelt spirit and professionalism, he was not discouraged by our pent up angers and fears of being intimate with people we really just met a few days ago. I learned a year later that all of the classes are dynamic (totally made for that specific class and moment) and it absolutely depends upon the progress being made as to when or even if intimacy can be explored on a physical level. Years ago when I was studying Ishinryu Karate, my teacher said that he would train us as hard as we allow ourselves to be trained. Truer words were never spoken for here also. There was a remarkable difference in levels and progress between the first year's course and the second time around. Because of the dynamics in play, it would be impossible and very disrespectful to discuss journeys in detail. We all had to bite our tongues so to speak to keep from answering other people's questions about what the sacred intimacy class is like. From my own experience, I found that once you mention the word "intimacy" that's all people seem to hear. They hear nothing else that follows and they even dismiss the word "sacred". Once intimacy is embedded in their minds, you might as well stop the conversation right there. All they hear, think and imagine is a class on how to have an orgy. Even a very well educated friend of mine who holds a doctorate degree told people that "Rocky's taking a course where he gets naked and has orgies." I was too ashamed to even sit with my friends at home after that statement. You can't possibly know the feelings and depth of spirit presented unless you are actually in class and in the moment. Nonetheless, the shallowness and immaturity of people on the outside never ceased to amaze me. On the other hand, I was looking from the inside out not the outside looking in. I'm curious, what did you first think of when your heard the term sacred intimacy?

I was doing fine within the course until my own anxiety surfaced. I was somewhat used to relating to women but when it came time to relate to men I was unduly afraid and confused. Eventually, I began to understand that touching the outside of the body in a non-sexual way such as softly stroking arms, back and legs was an excellent way to honor the nature of the person in front of you. When it was my turn to have the women caresses me, I felt I was truly honored for being male and honored for my nature. It was probably the closest thing to heaven I have ever truly experienced. Questions came to light the next day as the instructor continued to teach us. "What happens if . . . . You know . . . . If someone becomes excited in a sexual way during our journeys?" What if it does happen? How would you feel about his response? Should it really matter? Weather it happens or not, let the moment become what the moment is. Stay in the moment. The couple from South America got up and left at that point. Another couple decided to retreat to the extreme back of the classroom and actually built a wall out of unused chairs so they could journey in private or hide. No matter, it is what it is. I thought.

After dinner, we returned to class and without notice, during the current lecture, a small slight man stood up, removed his clothes and sat back down on the floor cushions. I couldn't help but stare like the rest of us when we were informed that by staring; we were not in the moment of the lecture. He was right again. It is so easy to be distracted by many things when you try to stay totally in the moment. Again, getting sky clad was never a requirement, only an invitation. By the next evening, we were all sky clad and guess what? Nobody gave it a second thought. No big deal at all. Just a few women were only topless due to biological reasons. If we didn't know each other before, we certainly knew each other now and that was mostly because of our continued expressions of emotions, wants, restrictions, needs, fears and alike. Learning to be open and face your fears is a very challenging journey to take.

CHAPTER TEN

Getting Burned by the Fire

My biggest regret the first year of class was not being able to "be here anyway". When faced directly with my own fears, I ran. I put on my clothes and made a bee line right into the woodlands. I didn't want to have anything to do with that class again. I was embarrassed, confused, hurt and just plain emotionally worn out. Fortunately for me, my teacher ran out of the classroom after me and confronted the situation. "Rocky, if you run out now and don't return to class, you will continue to run from your fears forever like I suspect you've always done in your life". Again, he was right on the money. When it gets too hot in the kitchen, I tend to run. This experience made it possible for me today to appreciate the swirling of thoughts my own students go through when journeying down this sacred path. Of course I returned to class even more embarrassed than before because due to my fast exit. It took an extreme amount of courage and trust in my instructor which he had certainly earned, to get started again. As it turned out, with the help of his two assistants things went well for the remainder of the course. I was so glad that I stayed with it. Not only did I learn about these sacred teachings but I no doubt learned to view a greater depth of my own being. Of course I still have deep seated regrets as to my running away so I decided to redeem myself by taking the course again the following year. I guess I was a bit overconfident about my redemption capabilities.

The second year was positively different than the first year. After our dancing and several journeys, we broke into smaller groups of five. The class was mainly against being sky clad so everyone was fully dressed all of time. We sat in circles of five with a spontaneous mixture of genders. As the instructor lectured, a young woman to the right of me leaned over and asked if I had taken the class last year. Yes I did, I whispered back. (After all we tried very hard not to be caught without having a total focus for the moment.) How far did it go? You know, did anybody actually have sex? I have to know, she said. I leaned over and again whispered. "The men made their own individual choices but the women in last year's class huddled together and made a collective consensus of their boundaries, I replied. Really? What did they decide? They decided that no matter what happens, there would be no penetration. That's what they decided as a unified group. PENETRATION? Did you say PENETRATION? She stood up, yelled penetration again as though bitten by a large spider, and proceeded to run out of the classroom right in the middle of our soulfully quiet lecture. The instructor declared it was break time, and then ran after her into the woods. Twenty minutes later, she and he returned. He announced that she had something to say to the class. I was ready to hide under my much too thin yoga pillow that I was sitting on. "I want to apologize for leaving class but that guy over there, I think his name is Rocky (pointing to me) is a sexual predator" she said loudly and definitively. Now I was ready to be shot by the nearest firearm. Please, somebody put me out of my misery I whispered under my breath while turning a bright shade of purple. Lucky for me the woman that I met and dined with for the last consecutive three days stood up and gave me a glowing and civil recommendation of my moral integrity. A lady from last year's class also stood up and vouched for my intentions. That night, I was seriously thinking of leaving the course again and actually started packing about 2:00am in the morning. I paused, took some deep breaths and decided that I would be more embarrassed if I didn't show up the next day. Besides, my teacher would have been proven right again if I indeed ran away for a second time.

Well, the class never did progress to even half of the journeys I took during the first year of studies. They were totally uptight. Too afraid and ashamed of their own bodies. They had no problem conveying their points of view though. Two days after my embarrassing encounter, the gentleman from Canada stood up and kindly faced the teacher saying "FUCK YOU" We were all motionless and in horror a second time. Our instructor was the kindest person I have ever met. His tone of voice was meek and reverent. He was always speaking of the divine and how we should all get along with each other. He certainly didn't deserve this again. His response to this intuitive outcry was even more shocking than I could have imagined. "Thank you for sharing that with me. I hope you take this course again next year to share more of your feelings with us." He quietly and very respectfully replied. It was only later on that I heard some of this students childhood fears were somehow stirred up and he could not confront them in peace. You see, we went deep, very deep indeed into the psyche of all of us So much love and respect burst forth from everyone and on occasion, so did the deeply seated fears and restrictions. We were so encouraged to feel and let everything out that some of us couldn't keep things hidden any longer. In the long run, I'm positive that everyone in the class is much better for it. By the time this course was over, I needed another vacation or at least three days of mindless eye candy.

It is becoming more difficult each year to teach this kind of course because of our growing religious restrictions and fears of intimacy. Certain institutions have banned the use of the words "clothing optional" in the course descriptions. We even had to sign a contract saying we were fully aware that the course is a clothing optional course, but now, even the contract is banned. This is a real tragedy of humankind. Do we take a shower blindfolded because our nudity is so offensive? The United States was one time viewed as being so progressive but is now totally shadowed by our European homeland that we left for "more freedom". So, sacred sex and real intimacy is needed even more today than yesterday. Our love, our human nature and respect for all that we are is starving from lack of attention as we continue to become robot like in our daily lives. Performance anxiety, adultery, Hollywood style sex, unrealistic expectations, lack of respect and starved marriages will continue on its present course unless we interject the divine and sacred in our life. We must learn to trust and open to our feelings and intrinsic human nature. Then can the divine, the sacred be invited into our beings and into our lovemaking.

CHAPTER ELEVEN

One Night in Heaven

I never thought I would experience such unconditional love without dying first but all of that changed one evening during class. Back in the first years' class, we were instructed to take our usual dinner break of about an hour and a half and then return to the small auditorium we used in the woods as our classroom. It was hinted somehow that we should return after dinner clean, refreshed and willing to be open with our classmates. We were all anxious and nervous at that point, but we also had a strong sense of a positive outcome. After all, this is what we had prepared for with many hours of consultations, questions and answers. This was going to be the culmination of many emotional and spiritual moments, the chance to actually experience the third dance, the divine and sacred intimacy. Tonight will be what all of the journeying and talk of acceptance was about. As the hour approached, I became more and more anxious. Perhaps everyone did. Throughout the course, the instructor had two assistants, one male and one female. They helped to fill in when the gender sides were uneven or if someone was having difficulty manifesting the journeys and walking the path. They turned out to be more professional and compassionate than I could have ever imagined.

As we entered our evening classroom, it was clear that everything had changed. This was not going to be a typical evening. The entire classroom was draped in very subtle candlelight. The windows were covered up with dark paper to keep any curiosity seekers away. In the center of the room was an extravagant tropical floral arrangement sitting on circular stepping stones. Subtle but fragrant floral incense emanated from the corners of the room. The wood floor was covered with a huge one inch thick blue mat that ran wall to wall. Soft East Indian music was playing in the background. Our mentor was sitting down at the front of the classroom on one of the multi-colored cushions that replicated themselves throughout the room. We were instructed to form groups of five and sit in a circle but this time time the genders must all be the same. As I joined a group of four men who seemed like great guys from what I learned of them, I glanced up to the front and saw Brian and Kelly, the two assistants. Kelly was drop dead gorgeous and was the envy of all the females in class. She had long flowing, shoulder length brown hair, piercing blue eyes, very fair colored skin and a body that had all the curves in the best places. Some women called her a voluptuous goddess. She was dressed in a ceremonial gown of blended floral colors that highlighted her form with stunning detail. Brian was dressed in white ceremonial pants and a long floral shirt. All of this was happening while being bathed in soft golden candlelight with the smell of sweet, earthy scents.

The instructor invited us to disrobe and move our clothes to the side walls. I did just that and then returned to the circle of five men. There were five or six circles in all. Some of all men, some of all women. The men's circles were on the left side of the room while the women were on the right side. The ceremony was to begin. One person from each of the circles would stand in the center of their own circle and invite the remaining people to caress them in a loving way for fifteen minutes. Then, they will step back into the circle and another person would take their place until everyone had the experience of being caressed. The person in the center could set their own boundaries and limits if they like and the rest must respect that without question. Some people had limits, others did not. Some preferred to lie down while others remained standing. Once this journey was complete we were then instructed to take one person from each circle and have two people from that circle escort (by holding hands) them to the opposite gender circle where they would stand and repeat the previous journey. After fifteen minutes, they are to be slowly and lovingly escorted back to their home circle by the opposite gender where they will then take someone else and repeat the journey until everyone was offered the experience in the opposite gender circle. Every time, we honored each other by using a Namaste greeting and holding our hands together in prayer and bowing slightly with the highest respect for the lovely person in front of us. We bowed again before leaving the center of the circle. Kelly and Brian joined in their respective circles where the numbers weren't complete. I have never felt more respected as a person in my life. This was unconditional love with the highest respect with divine natures than I could have ever imagined. Everyone was loved. Everyone was blessed with a return to their own primal nature, their authentic human nature. We were all in the moment, making each second sacred and caring as much as possible for the well being of each other. It was truly a night in which the sacred third dance was present. It could not have been more perfect. I thank my mentor for that. It is quite a job to facilitate and supervise a group of people while creating a safe and sacred place for loving.

In my limited observation of other circles, I noticed in general that the women were more uninhibited in caressing other women than the men were with their own gender. I know I was challenged in my feelings. What would my mamma say? What would pop (Mr. Machismo) do to me if he found out about this? How can I let guys touch my naked arms and legs? Oh the horror and dishonor. As my thoughts began to betray me, I slowly breathed in and then breathed out in total surrender until my primal nature took over and I was returned to being in the moment. Although I feel the men were challenged in this way, the women were challenged when they were escorted into the circle of men. Thoughts of sexual abuse and childhood trauma may have clouded one woman's thoughts and interfered with her moments of sacredness. To my recollection, only one female was unable to deal with the journey and she bowed out to sit on the sidelines. She wept. From a caring perspective, I went to console her after the journey was over but she was not to be consoled and remained weeping for an undisclosed reason. Some people had cultural baggage and I believe that this was one of those people. Kelly was well aware of the situation and sat down beside her and just held her in a maternal embrace for what seemed to be about forty-five minutes. I have the highest respect for Kelly. Her compassionate and professional nature was amazing. She was truly divine and goddess like. I'm still in contact with Kelly from time to time. She has since branched out and began her own practice traveling the world over devoting her life to helping people reach a higher spiritual level.

So, the question is, what are you feeling right now? Did the previous journey offend you? What would you do in following the same path? What restrictions pop up? Are you haunted by religious condemnation or same sex prejudices? Perhaps the "oh my God, what would my mamma say?" came to light. All of that and more surfaced for me so don't be ashamed if it did for you too. NO! You don't have to do this journey. This was just my account of my own personal journey. The good news is that by learning to be in the moment, all of our "stuff" will begin to dissolve. I mention the word learn as an oxymoron. Unfortunately we need to learn it but in reality it's just a return to who we really are and who we were really meant to be. We were meant to be ourselves and not someone else's expectations of whom they believe we should be. I invite you now to return home. Re-visit the human side. Come home now and begin to celebrate all that you are and the true nature of your spiritual path will be revealed. Namaste.

CHAPTER TWELVE

Breaking the Myth of Dualism

In my continued spiritual studies, I was introduced to the concept of dualism and its function in humanity. Many modern religions preach the gospel of good and evil, heaven and hell, animal or human, right or wrong, perfection or fault. These religious disciplines have embraced the concept of dualism and by doing so denying us of the erotic and assertive parts of our basic human nature They perpetuate and strive for human perfection. They believe we should all be perfect in every way. After all, is not God (Spirit, Krishna, Jesus, Gandhi, Buddha and others) perfect? In their doctrine to strive for perfection they ask us to evolve and rise above our basic instincts, our humanism. They hope that we may gravitate to the image of saintliness. In many cases, by denying our basic instincts the results will be less than optimum and may even manifest itself in less than desirable acts. Local and national religious leaders struggle with this very concept on just about a daily basis. Perhaps you've seen them in the news. The clergy who purport to be celibate are not necessarily immune to their

46

own sexual needs. Indeed history confirms that the dualistic concept of good or evil fueled the unspeakable acts of violence in the name of God during the Spanish inquisition, the Crusades and the Salem witch trials. In coming home to our own natural spiritual path, we recognize our basic instincts and therefore strive for balance and wholeness instead of perfection. In doing so we can now add something to the dualism and expand it just a bit. The ancient druids believed in the power of the triad which incorporates instinct, humanism and divine spirit. In viewing the triple Celtic knot work, we see that each of part of the triad is not only connected to each other, but interwoven in a pattern having no beginning and no ending. Isn't that a more realistic way for daily living in harmony than fruitlessly striving for perfection? May I ask, what happens if you don't reach daily perfection at home, in your sexuality, or at the workplace? Could this be the basis of guilt and regret? Is it possible that these feelings may indeed keep us from being in the moment and really savoring all that is given to us by the divine? Even our educational system perpetuates the myth of dualism. Surprisingly so does religion, race and ethnic origins. You're either Catholic or you're not. You are saved by Jesus or you're not. You won the race or you didn't. You wrote the correct answers in school or you're wrong. We are African American or we're Caucasian and on it goes.

Let go of your logical or illogical thinking and dualistic beliefs. Sacred intimacy grows when we are in touch with all that is and maybe even all that can be. Aim for wholeness as described by the ancient druidic spiritualists. Embrace your humanism and full sexuality, your basic instincts. Feel and love again in all of its glory and splendor. Always do so in the spirit of respect, caring and love. It does not matter to me what label of sexuality you choose, but know that the best label is simply no label at all. We need not be afraid of anything that we feel in a loving way because it is all God given. Everything we are is God given. Let us now come home and celebrate all that we are.

CHAPTER THIRTEEN

Exercises for Building a Strong Foundation for Intimacy

Cognitive Journeying:

1. Let go of all pre-conditions
2. Release any notion of expectations of sexual performance
3. Drop all constrictive religious beliefs
4. Free yourself of worthless parental expectations
5. Learn to turn off your robotic self and enter the world of natural feelings
6. Strive for wholeness not perfection

Physical Journeying:

1. Be totally in the moment.
2. Breathe in slowly to feel more and then slowly exhale as you surrender to the
3. Breathe less if you want to feel less.
4. Close your eyes if you need mental space or to be more with yourself.
5. Relax and let your body move in its' natural rhythms.
6. If possible, cleanse the body and relax the mind in preparation for the divine.
7. There is no "right" or "wrong", only wholeness, respect and openness.
8. You always retain the right to alter the experience if you feel in danger or harm.
9. Journeying is by invitation and never a requirement
10. The eyes are the windows to the soul. Use all of your senses for a rich experience.

Afterwards:

1. Keep the sacred spaces sacred. Do not turn your space in to a garage littered with things that distract the moment.
2. Discussion and communication is always helpful but never confront others in anger about what was said, done or revealed during the journey. Yes, you may learn something new about your partner and many new things about yourself, however never accuse, argue with, challenge or embarrass anyone for their willingness to be fully open to you. It's the quickest path to closing doors that were opened in love and good faith.
3. Remember to simply honor your significant other or participants before and after with a simple thank you, blessing or folded hands with a Namaste bow. When you honor your partner in this way, you honor their nature and the divine third dance of sacred intimacy.

CHAPTER FOURTEEN

The Surprise

The surprise is that it's not really about sex. Sex has nothing to do with it. It's just that sexual relations provide a readily available and seductively inviting door in which to enter the here and now. Music, dance, vacations, driving, loving, interacting, meditating, yoga, and experiencing life with all of our senses puts us into the sacred, into this moment. I had a recent experience and good lesson from Dan Millman (Way of the Peaceful Warrior). He invited me to come to a lecture he was giving in King of Prussia, Pa. for a health and wellness expo. Afterwards we had the opportunity to walk around visiting most of the exhibitors. I am in awe of Dan and really appreciated the fact he gave me some personal time when so many other people wanted his time too. We stopped at a booth where a man was demonstrating the health benefits of a "super powerful" wonder blender. He was mixing various whole fruits and giving out some free samples. The line for samples was getting pretty long so I took advantage of the time to ask Dan an important question. I asked Dan "Out of all the things you have accomplished in life so far, what's your next biggest life goal? To say his answer surprised me is an understatement. "To get a free sample of that blended juice" he replied. Enough said and lesson learned. I was thinking of the future and not appreciating the present moment. By now we can conclude that many things put us into the moment. It doesn't have to be limited to sex. Once our minds are clear, we can allow ourselves to feel throughout the body, using the senses. In sacred sex, the key is to feel, not think, however can you imagine what daily living would be like if we combined clear thinking with a heightened awareness of the five senses? Stay with me here. Our greatest gift given to us by the divine is life itself. Life is consumed by a series of moments that are not unlimited. They are finite. If life is truly a blessing from above, wouldn't that also make each moment sacred? Of course it does. Every moment that you experience is a blessing, the blessing of life that is given to all. The question is; do we personally savor each moment as a blessing? If we did, we wouldn't waste our moments being angry, vengeful, depressed and so on. In relationships, how many divorcees literally still hate each other? How many couples still have deep seated secrets that remain hidden in their marriage? How many parents harbor resentment because their son or daughter is gay is not successful or was born with a lifelong disease? It is because most of us have not come home in our daily lives or maybe we made the journey home but there is no one there. Most haven't yet realized that the only way to be here now is to be in a spirit of love. My mentor calls these people "heart felt" because they feel more love and stay in the sacredness of the moment. If everyone were heart felt there would be no more war or a need for equal rights or crime and punishment.

O.K. now you're probably thinking that I'm fantasizing about an un-obtainable, idealistic society right? Well, concerning sacred intimacy and relationships, we witnessed that being in the moment enhances and changes relationships for the better. Therefore, part of the surprise is that it works just as well out of the bedroom too. The next step and the next challenge is to transmute sacred moments into our daily living routine. When this is accomplished, every day, every moment is a blessing regardless if it is a good moment or bad. Remember the story about the man from Canada earlier on? Our teacher could not have responded the way he did to the man's shouted obscenities if he were not "here now" in the spirit of love and respect. So, the next time you experience road rage or other offenses against your nature, absorb it in the spirit of love and render it helpless by realizing even THIS is a gift, the gift of another moment of life. From a worldly view, we can't be responsible for the lives of everyone but we can be responsible for ourselves. Simply be the love that you want to see in others and it will set in motion a chain of blessed manifestation. It all has to begin somewhere, let it begin now, in this moment . . . with YOU.

Journey: Expressing Your Desires

In this journey, sit down on the floor with your partner facing you. Cross the legs in an "X" position and touch the ankles into your body. Sit close enough to your partner that your knees are touching their knees. Clear your mind. Be sure the room is prepared in subdued lighting with soft, slow exotic music playing in the background. Take each other's hands and look directly into the eyes of your partner. Repeat the following words together at the same time. "I want; I love; I need; I desire." Repeat it softly many times until you feel the emotions and implications of every word. Next, close your eyes and repeat the journey again, this time tapping into you deep inner feelings. Finally, open your eyes again and convey these deep inner feelings to your partner. Being seen on the inside is vital to this journey. Use your eyes as windows revealing hidden emotions. Hide nothing. Be open and the love that you are. Celebrate the coming together of two souls meeting as one. Be joyous in melding together. Afterwards, end the journey by joining together in a heartfelt embrace. Take as much time as you both need. Stay in the moment and rejoice. It will be easier now to express your desires verbally than it was before. Feel free to add more to the mantra and customize it as the need arises. It can be tailored to lovemaking where inner and previously hidden desires can blossom in the sacred spaces created by both of you. Be specific and emotionally expressive in customizing each mantra. The more specific and heartfelt you are, the richer the journey will be.

CHAPTER FIFTEEN

You Belong to Me?

Growing up in an entertainment rich society, most of us have heard the term "You Belong to me". In dating, we want the other person to be ours. In marriage, we want our soul mate to be ours for the rest of our lives. Could this also be a part of a faux foundation for love? After all, once we say "I do" we can forget about being nice, dressing well, and honoring our partner with the same intensity as we did when we were single. Why? Well, because the law says that you belong to me until death do we part. We've accomplished our goal. We snagged our partner into a hopefully unbreakable legal and clerical bond. No matter what I do or don't do, they are mine forever. They belong to me and me only. For the females, it may manifest itself in the way of a decrease in meal preparations and table settings, quality time spent with your partner or even a decrease in intimacy and sexual bonding. Frequently males witness less appealing wardrobes in the females too. The beautiful lace covered, see through lingerie has been replaced by a gray jogging suit. Hair color slowly fades into the past while weight gain is forever on the increase.

Women may see males home less frequently or see an increase in escape tactics such as working later, drinking more, smoking more, or even drug use. They may experience stressful conversations or even confrontations about money, sex, children or in-laws. Of course there are many different ways that a lack of sacred intimacy can manifest itself in relationships. The foundation for these unfortunate events unfolding is what I call the "You belong to me" syndrome. This is the foundation of expectancy where demands are sprouted faster than weeds in a garden. One of the most common manifestations of expectancy is infidelity. A typical scenario for both partners (male or female) is that you can't look at any other person even in an innocent but interested way. You can't dance with anyone else, look at pictures of anyone else, fantasize or have any desire to socialize with anyone but your partner. Did someone say the word jealousy? Jealousy grows out of a lack of trust which in turn sprouts from a lack of sacred intimacy. It's all connected. When it was suggested that a young couple consider the idea of journeying with other classmates besides their own partner they were appalled. Again, no one is required to do anything at all, but the invitation was on the table so to speak. For the most part, they stayed together but did journey occasionally with others. A wonderful outcome to all of this is that at the end of the course, they announced their engagement. I believe they learned the concept that we don't own anyone, not our partner, our soul mate or anyone else. We are all part of the collective universe. By insisting that you own your partner or significant other, you are setting the stage for unrealistic expectations, stress and infidelity. By honoring our partner, we create an unbreakable foundation for love through respect and praise instead of by demand and requirements. If you are male, and this concept makes you feel less of a man, then your male ego is getting in the way of your relationship. If you are female, you will find that by opening and honoring each other, the relationship will solidify into something they cannot possible get anywhere else. Certainly it pales in comparison to just having typical sex. As you both can see, there are so many benefits and so much ecstatic joy that can come from creating sacred intimacy. You may choose to journey only with your partner and that's wonderful. Explore experiment, communicate without words or with words but always communicate by opening and honoring each other.

CHAPTER SIXTEEN

Be Playful and Experiment

Loving someone by being totally focused and in the moment is always a celebration. Be playful, open and try new things. Remember you will not be judged or harmed in any way when journeying in the spirit of love and respect. Laugh and have fun. Release playfulness and joy in every interaction. Smile, open your eyes and open your inner self. Touch in such a way that it expresses your inner respect and honor for the other persons nature. Breathe into the touching and breathe out the surrender of "I am." Once you've experienced the pure joy of having created something truly beautiful and unique, you will probably want to include sacred intimacy as part of your life from that point on. Other types of preparations and accessories are free for the trying. As you become more playful and more open to each other, you may wish to journey sans clothing, inside or outside in a natural and safe setting. There is nothing quite like being sky clad (naked) in nature on a warm summer day or by a roaring fire or even by a lake. Let yourself enjoy nature the natural way as it was meant to be enjoyed. Even a well manicured back yard can do nicely (if the neighbors are not too close). Feel the wetness of the grass. Smell the natural scents of the good green earth. Hear the birds and wildlife celebrate with you as you are both bathed in gentle moonlight.

Perhaps this is not available to you if you live in a city, but there are many places that provide cabins in the woods. Many resorts are beautiful places also. If you're stuck in the city, a fireplace and earthy scented candles will do nicely. Perhaps just a stroll hand in hand while being in the moonlight (with clothes) and glancing at the stars above can stimulate a return to nature. Be creative. Look for an opportunity to bring nature inside your domain. Even a pine tree or houseplants with a little electronic fountain can somewhat replicate a nature like setting. When we return to nature, we connect with the earth in a basic and prehistoric way. It is a way that reminds us to feel, see and touch all the beauty that surrounds us. Creating sacred intimacy with the help of nature reinforces our basic instincts and helps us to open up and honor all that is. We've grown accustomed to concrete, steel, plastics and artificial lighting. Our human nature craves a connection from which we have progressively forgotten. It's not too late to re-connect with our natural selves, our sexual selves. Just a few minutes in nature every day is a great way to begin. Take a walk in the park. Touch a tree and feel the energy within it. Glance at the stars. Walk along the ocean and catch the rhythm of the waves. Claim what is naturally yours and make it a part of your nature. It may seem like a long journey home but it begins with just a few minutes each day. Even if the only thing possible is to touch a houseplant or to sit down on a patch of grass, do it! The rewards are tremendous just in stress relief alone. Nature is part of all of us. Return to it in joy and playfulness. Add it to the sacred intimacy that we've created all along. Become the fully open and sensuous human you were meant to be.

Journey into playfulness

In this journey we will return to playfulness and sexiness. Set up the evening for free style dancing. This time, add a blindfold to highlight the other senses and create an atmosphere of mystery. Begin by free dancing as you have before. On this path, use both medium speed exotic music followed by slower music (but still rhythmic). Use the faster dances to return to your primal nature and to prepare your soul for what is to follow. When the music changes to a slower pace, face each other and add sensual pelvic thrusts and other movements to highlight your gender and attract the person opposite you. Slowly move closer to one another until almost touching while slowly dancing the dance of man or woman. Continue for several minutes and then one person should put on the blindfold. And remain in place. The other person can now sensuously dance around the person with the blindfold, touching and enticing them with every step. Exchange the blindfold and repeat the journey awakening the senses to all that is within you. Play, tease, entice, bite, nibble, lick and have fun bringing the natural sexiness to life in both of you. This can be done with just one couple or several at a time.

CHAPTER SEVENTEEN

Looking at the world of Sacred Intimacy

In researching and learning about sacred intimacy, I found many different doctrines, styles, methods and techniques. Tantra seems to have become an increasingly popular word. Tantric sex has more definitions than I care to list or even consider here. Tantra to me simply means "all that is" (in a conceptual view). In promoting sacred sex and intimacy, most practitioners create a path of sexual techniques, and therefore the journeys are about sexual techniques also. They emphasize locating the "G" spot, how to caress the yoni and other methods to deliver heart pounding orgasms. Websites tout the pursuit of orgasm as the alpha and omega of sacred sex and use the word Goddess much too often.

I beg to differ from this path and these journeys. Our path is focused on sacred intimacy via the door of sacred sex, music, food and even life. It should not be about sexual technique because that's where the mystery comes in, where the "ah ha" happens and where the sacred resides. It lives in the magic of feelings and being more human. Sexual techniques only produce predictable outcomes, therefore keeping us from being in the moment. The Kama Sutra shows many different sexual positions and I've heard couples speak about doing positions number twelve through fifteen the next time they make love. Too many popular women's magazines also tout the latest in techniques. ("How to light his fire like never before (technique # 4) There is no need for sexual techniques except perhaps from a clinical or therapeutic view, or if you are diligently pursuing the mighty orgasm. I would suggest that we shift our focus to also include feelings and a swift return to our nature and all of nature in general. Returning home is all we need to do to have a spiritual path to sacred intimacy. With that being said, it reminds me of a quote that was said to me by Dan Millman (author: way of the Peaceful Warrior) "There only one light, but many lamps." And so it is with Tantra, intimacy and sacred sex.

Another interesting perspective is looking at all of this from the word "permission". I remember hearing a sex therapist on television say "I spent my entire life giving permission for people to feel good." I think she's right. Isn't it amazing that we need someone else's authority to allow us to do what is perfectly natural, to do what is God given and divine? This is proof on how far we have let us drift into a multi-tasking, robotic state of consciousness. There are too many places in the world where sexual sins and other forms of denials exist. We hear about them constantly and without pause. Seldom are we encouraged to be in the moment, to explore all of our sensual delights with abandon and playfulness. Do you need permission to be all you can be? If you do, it's because the world has stifled intimacy as something sinful or something unacceptable. Don't you believe it. Get the prohibitive clergy and religious dogma out of your head if there is no encouragement to develop sacred intimacy from it. There are so many other things to need permission for, let's not allow it invade the sanctity of love between anybody.

CHAPTER EIGHTEEN

Questions from my Students

Q. Is sacred intimacy better between a committed couple in love or as part of group?

A. It really isn't a question of better or worse (remember duality?) it's just different. The advantage of sacred intimacy with two people in a loving relationship is that over a period of time they begin to understand each other more deeply. They may feel safer and thereby open up more completely. The disadvantage is that expectancy might be created subconsciously leading to unrealistic future expectations and disappointments. Keeping things new and fresh has sometimes been a challenge for long term couples.

Q. How are things different for same sex couples?

A. For our classes, there's not much of a difference. We do speak about being male and being female however since parts of both genders can reside within the same body, they can relate to each other as they wish. Personally, it does not matter which gender, you are or you associated with. I don't put a label on people.

Q. What if I'm too shy to remove my clothing with my current partner or in a classroom?

A. The purpose of removing clothing is to visually and psychologically assist in opening up to your nature. The purpose is really to be totally open with others whether or not clothing is worn. It is always by invitation and never a requirement.

Q. How do I cope with my anxiety and shyness in relating to others?

A. Welcome all of your feelings as a part of the gift of life. Close your eyes and be with just yourself for a few moments. Breathe in slowly and breathe out into the surrender. When you feel more comfortable, open your eyes and partake in the moment.

Q. I'm afraid that if I really open up to my partner, they will reject my feelings. How can I keep from being hurt emotionally?

A. If both people are present in the divine spirit of love, there is no judging, labeling or condemnation. Open up and use your heart to guide both of you.

Q. You use the terms sacred intimacy and sacred sex interchangeably. Why?

A. Because they are so closely related. It is sacred sex that can create a window or path to sacred intimacy. They are not the same thing however. One is the window/door and the other is the path.

Q. I've studied Tantric Sex for many years; can't we skip the honoring and get to the good stuff?

A. Maybe you should study a bit longer and re-examine your experiences.

Q. What would my priest or rabbi say if they found out that I was taking this course?

A. The purpose of religion is to give us a path to take where there is no path. In present doctrines, the path has been veering far from our basic instincts and human nature. It has been dominated by what they define as "sin" and "redemption" (the dualist theory). In the case with Catholicism, man is even born with an automatic sin. Our human nature is not supported or encouraged, yet it is said that the true kingdom of God is within you. If this is so, then our basic human nature can indeed lead a path to the divine.

Q. What about orgasm?

A. By my definition (and others) orgasm can be translated to mean "too much." It is the body's response to over stimulation that creates a release. The problem with orgasms is that it has become the sole purpose of intimacy and sex with most everyone. They believe that there can be no satisfaction without achieving orgasm. Indeed, that's what is most popular in pornography. Everybody wants to see the ultimate in physical satisfaction via the orgasm. When this is our only goal for having sex, we soon find that our orgasm lasts only seconds and there is no long term sacred intimacy happening, only a shell of an anemic physical experience. When orgasm is not achieved, doubt, suspicion and disappointment are created because the destination has not been reached. The solution is that we should be concerned with a satisfying and divine journey, not just the destination. It is the sacred intimacy that is created during sex that will nourish our souls and create an unbreakable bond between our partner and ourselves. This is what will keep marriages together and relationships solid; not the quest for orgasm. Imagine our goal was to not be hungry for food, so we just eat loaves of bread and drink a quart of water with the notion that we need to feel full. It can easily be done by everyone, but should it be done? I think not. Suppose we ate the bread as fast as we can to get that "full" feeling as quick as possible? This path only helps to distract us even more from the joys of sacred intimacy. There should never be a rush to an intimate destination. In fact, why should there be a destination at all? Let go and let the path take you where it will with no expectations or requirements. Feel, enjoy and rejoice in your divine primal nature.

Q. Our work schedules are crazy. We have no time for all of this. Can't we just do an occasional quickie? Besides doesn't the planning take out all of the spontaneity?

A. A quickie can be sacred too, if you both let go of the conscious mind, respect each other and just feel what is.

Q. My wife and I have been active in the B&D lifestyle (bondage and discipline) and we both love it! What do you have to say about that?

A. Great. You may want to consciously focus on adding sacred intimacy to the mix.

CHAPTER NINETEEN

Unlocking the Code

The success and celebrations that come from The Joy of Sacred Intimacy is unlocked with just three words; Patience; Openness and Respect. Let's take look at each one. Without patience there is a tendency to rush to the finish line and encourage selfishness. There might even be some disrespect along the way because the focus is on the destination and not on the journey. I believe that where sacred intimacy is concerned; reaching the end quickly denies you and your partner the main purpose of doing this at all, which is the celebration of the interactions during the journey. It is the interactions (the intimacy) that we are truly missing in our lives (verbal, spiritual and physical). A lack of patience can cause disappointment by providing expectations of time. Openness and honesty is missing in relationships also. To be here, in the moment and with complete openness and honesty is to truly be present in love. Most people cannot be truly open and honest with their partners or even spouses because we are told to keep to ourselves or lie to keep from being hurt. Being open is not just about being open with the past but being open to the full range of possibilities in the moment. The mantra needs to change from "not this or this or this or even that; to this, and this and that." Open into the moment and into the infinite, divine possibilities of all that is. Respect for yourself and for partners or spouse is the key ingredient in honoring. By honoring, I mean respecting the intrinsic nature of the other person. Remember that both of you are giving the most precious thing you have together, and that is "this moment". It can never be captured the exact same way again. Our life is of a dynamic nature. We need to respect the moment given to us and thank them, the divine and ourselves for the participation, openness and joy shared. These words are the codes to unlocking the future on the path to a solid relationship, and to sacred intimacy.

Journey: Listening to the spirit:

In this journey, we are developing our attentiveness by just listening to man and woman speak. This can be done within a group just between two partners. If between partners, sit comfortably across from each other on the floor. One partner is to speak for about five minutes about anything on their mind while the other partner just listens attentively. The key here is for the silent partner not to speak at all, not even one word. Make no comments, gestures or corrections. Just listen until the other person if finished fully. Then, repeat the exercise with the opposite partner. Open up completely. Let your emotions flow in divine communication. There are no barriers or taboo subjects. There is no right or wrong topic or subject, only pure communication. Enjoy the moment. For groups, have the women sit in a small, tight circle in the center of the room while the men sit in a larger circle around the women. Let the women have a group conversation about what's on their minds while the men just sit patiently and listen attentively. Then, reverse the group now with the men in the center and the women listening on the outside. This is a great journey for finding out more about our partners feelings as men or women.

CHAPTER TWENTY

Adding Blessings

You may want to add verbal blessings before and after journeying. If the thought of saying blessings is a frightening thought, think of it as sharing positive vibrations from you and the divine with your partner. At the beginning of the journey, it may be a blessing about staying in the moment; It could also be a blessing for the room to be a sacred space. It can really be anything you want it to be in sharing your feelings merged with the divine and spirit. Blessings can resemble prayer in some ways in that it asks for positive energy and trust. After the journey is complete, perform a blessing of thanks and praise. You may even take turns sharing blessings between partners, groups or with a significant other. Experiment from the heart and ask the divine spirit to enter and share with you. Here is an example of an opening blessing for beginning journeys. Feel absolutely free to change the words in any way that suits you or better yet, just speak from the heart and keep it completely in the moment.

Opening Blessing:

I call upon the divine goddess to join us on this sacred and celebrated journey. May our hearts open in the spirit of love as we learn about each other and bond together in joy.

It's sometimes more intimate to hold hands when saying the blessings and perhaps bowing with the "Namaste" for the blessing at the journeys' end. Take a few moments now to gather your thoughts and just feel the divine spirit within you. By including blessings, you honor all that is and keep the people and places sacred and special. When teaching, I always invite the divine spirit but preface it by saying the divine can be represented by whomever you want it to. This includes but is not limited to Buddha, God, Jesus, Krishna, Goddess, Gaia, the Holy Spirit, Awen, Saints, Mystics, Crone or the collective universe. What matters is the invitation and intention.

By now you should be able to see a distinctive difference between the status quo and sacred intimacy. I hope that it is clear as to which one will bring you the most joy, playfulness and spiritual fulfillment.

CHAPTER TWENTY ONE

The Role of Nature

Like it or not, we are all connected in some ways and are part of this planet in which we reside. My mantra is "Nature Nurtures". We retreat to nature by taking vacations where there is sun and trees or snow and water. The role nature plays in our well being is just now coming to light as a serious course of study. Eco-psychology can now be found as part of many university campuses. Yet, this is the same philosophies used for thousands of years by the Druids and other Pagan groups. Nature is a part of being human and it will always be so. It refreshes us, heals us and sustains us. We touched upon these thoughts earlier in this book but it should be emphasized that to deny us nature is to deny us of our humanism. Make nature a part of your path to intimacy. Use its beauty to enrich the senses of exotic smells and sights. Learn to become more human instead of more robotic in everyday life. Nature is honored by having it partake in your journeys. Even today, nature is used subliminally to touch our hearts and awaken us. Most television infomercials and even televangelists use a background of palm trees, fountains, the beach or a variety of exotic plants during interviews and testimonials. Why? Because it touches us in our deepest places where our basic human nature resides. We see it and gravitate to it. It relaxes us and keeps our attention (movement). It keeps us in the moment while silently calling us home. These are powerful and seductive relationships which sells millions of products each year. However, used properly they can enhance and bless our concrete cocoons we call home or even office. Humans were not meant to live in steel and concrete away from the very land which nourishes us. Neither were they meant to have anemic sexual relationships that they call intimate. It doesn't work anymore. Hollywood still believes differently however, and as parenting responsibility and skills diminish, the video games, television, cell phones, internet and iPods become more of the primary source of relationship information. Only by returning to nature and embracing our human nature can we reverse the trend for ourselves, our children and the future of all.

CHAPTER TWENTY TWO

Another Point of View

I am amazed at how many instructors and goddesses there are teaching some form of intimacy or sacred sex. I continued my studies a few years ago by enrolling into another relationship class, this time by a well known relationship expert and speaker. It was so ironic when I found out that my colleague Kelly was taking the class too. We met up and decided to take the classes together. It was a weekend course with about one hundred and twenty people attending. The class was held in a medium sized auditorium with the typical folding chairs filling the room. In a nutshell, the day was spent describing and evaluating everyone's physical attractiveness. In one of our journeys, the men were to be rated by the women on their appearance and sexual potential. Out of about seventy five men, only three were rated a zero. I was one of them. If I had a pistol, I would have used it on myself without hesitation. I was too embarrassed for words. I turned toward Kelly but she was mixed in with some other section of the auditorium. One of the zero guys (not me) raised their hand and asked if the men could have a chance to rate the women in the same way. "Positively Not" the instructor roared back with militant authority. He explained why. "If any of the women were rated a zero, they would be traumatized for weeks and probably never return to this class again." I just couldn't understand why it was o.k. for the men to get a chance to feel bad. We adjourned for lunch and Kelly and I had a chance to talk a bit. She was just as appalled as I was. I think it's because we were both used to always talking about love, respect, honoring and compassion. We returned to class after lunch and the subject was still about understanding the physical attractiveness between men and women. It seemed much too superficial for either of us (Kelly and I). By the end of the day though, people were becoming more intrigued with what they can do to look more appealing and attract a mate. The suggestions were made by a consensus so I guess it made sense after all. I did end up learning more than I expected about sexual attractiveness, but the previous embarrassment factor kicked in and the mantra "be here now, be here anyway" was fighting for dominance within me. I just couldn't seem to reconcile with the fact that I paid for a course that made me feel embarrassed and dejected. Kelly stayed for the next day, but I had my fill for the time being and used the following day to reflect of the previous days' events and what they meant to me and to others. So, I guessed I could have done better with the "being here now, be here anyway" part, but at least I recognized that it was still something for me to overcome. To this day it is still a challenge for me every now and then but not as often as it was just a few years ago. It's all part of being human and in reality, all a blessed experience. The point is simply that many people have different ideas about love, tantric, intimacy and sexual relationships. The lamp that I carry may not illuminate the path for you, but I encourage you to keep seeking a lamp that will do just that. I would make one suggestion though; look within and learn to trust your own feelings and intuition while being open and respectful to all that is. Trusting your feelings with intimacy can be done by simply being open and keenly aware as to what creates a feeling of innocence, playfulness and love. We somehow know what is potentially pleasurable even when journeying into secret places where we've never been before. And so the journey continues.

CHAPTER TWENTY THREE

Putting it all Together

Your journeys may be the same or different than the ones mentioned here. Sacred intimacy can even be two people just falling asleep in each others' arms. Why? Because the experience is genuine, open, respectful, coessential and totally in the moment. It will take a bit of determination and patience to go from metropolitan, western sexual relationships to one that includes sacred intimacy. The journey can be one of playfulness, fun, satisfaction and most importantly one of solidarity. It's not the sex that holds us together in a heartfelt bond, it's the intimacy. Don't forget that sacred intimacy can be opened through many windows. Tasting new food together for the first time is a window also. Food has been a sensual part of living for quite a long time. Today, we sometimes prepare an exotic dinner for a new date or special occasion. We may even go out to dinner as a preface for the sexual intimacy to come. For me, I've always appreciated food more when I or someone took the time to prepare it with care. There is something very sacred about preparing food. It's like putting a little of each of us with every part of the recipe. I'm not a cook for sure, but even the act of preparing a cup of real green tea, using just the leaves (no tea bag) and a special small tea container keeping the purified water at the perfect temperature, was quite an experience. For the first time, I took pride in preparing my food, even if was just a cup of green tea. The taste was very rewarding enhanced by the fact that I took the time and focus to prepare it properly. It certainly beats going out to the local diner where there would be no preparation or care at all.

Simple life experiences, shared with a significant other or partner can be another window into the sacred. For example, when I teach adult courses (business, self development, and leadership) at the local colleges, I try to give my students a unique experience that would not be found anywhere else. It may be that I'm animated to the max, it may be a unique video, and it may be me telling some very lame jokes (yes, very lame indeed). Whatever it is, the students can now relate to one another their impressions of the unique experiences that happened during our class time. Shouldn't be the same idea with our partners or even just ourselves? Most of go on vacation or holiday once or twice a year. It is at that time when we can share those unique intimate experiences, but what about everyday life? Are we just focused on being together for vacation time? Could that be the beginning of getting into a typical routine of working toward a vacation salvation? Why? Every moment with our partner can be something special and unique if we want it to be. It is said that women like getting flowers for no special reason, just because. Why? Because it is an act that was done in the moment without obligation and with respect and love. It was sacred. We appreciate when the gift of time is given because it the most precious gift of all. A greeting card is nice, but a gift of time and focus is much better. Our loved ones and even ourselves appreciate the gift of time more than anything else. Our lifetime partner, family and parents would all be thankful if we could just be in the moment with them creating a once in a lifetime gift of sacred intimacy. There is so much beauty in life. We only go around once in this world. Why not make each moment precious? Let the change in this world and in your relationships begin today, now, in this moment with you.

Bright Blessings to you,
R Romeo

END NOTES

I would love to hear your successful experiences on the path of sacred intimacy. There will be a follow up book outlining successful couples and their journeys. If you wish to anonymously share your journeys, send them in confidence to the email address below. Also, feel free to contact me if I can be of service to your relationship or your organization. I really enjoy speaking to groups and working with enlightened people.

R. Romeo
rockyr@earthlink.net

Don't forget to order your FREE additional Sacred Intimacy Journeys (a $59.00 value). Just send your request to *rockyr@earthlink.net* and they will be emailed to you quickly.

CPSIA information can be obtained at www.ICGtesting.com
Printed in the USA
BVOW08s0716150516

448139BV00003B/205/P